Knights

Laura Durman

ARCTURUS

This edition first published in 2012 by Arcturus Publishing

Distributed by Black Rabbit Books
P. O. Box 3263
Mankato
Minnesota MN 56002

Printed in China

Library of Congress Cataloging-in-Publication Data

Durman, Laura.
  Knights / by Laura Durman.
     p. cm. -- (Knights and castles)
  Includes index.
  ISBN 978-1-84858-561-4 (hbk. : library bound)
  1. Knights and knighthood--Juvenile literature. 2. Civilization, Medieval--Juvenile literature. I. Title.
  CR4509.D87 2013
  940.1--dc23
                            2011051452

Series Concept: Discovery Books Ltd.
www.discoverybooks.net
Editor for Discovery Books: Laura Durman
Designer: Ian Winton

Picture credits: Corbis: 18 (The Print Collector), 23 (The Gallery Collection), 28 (Fred de Noyelle / Godong); Peter Dennis: 5, 7b, 11, 16; Getty Images: pp 6 (The Bridgeman Art Library / French School), 8 (The Bridgeman Art Library / Italian School), 9 (Alfredo Dagli Orti / The Art Archive), 15 (Johannes Simon / Staff), 19 (The Bridgeman Art Library / Sir Frank Dicksee), 24 (Bridgeman Art Library / Sir John Everett Millais), 29t (Courtesy of Museum of M.D. Mallorca; Ramon Manent); Adam Hook: 22; Photoshot: 26 (STARSTOCK); Shutterstock Images: cover (Raulin), pp 4 (rosesmith), 7t (Sakala), 10 (Sakala), 12 (FXQuadro), 13 (Robert H Creigh), 20 (alexsol), 21 (PLRANG), 25 (sergign), 29b (akva); Warwick Castle: 17; Wikimedia Commons: 14, 27 (Jules Eugène Lenepveu / Tijmen Stam).

Every attempt has been made to clear copyright. Should there be any inadvertent omission, please apply to the publisher for rectification.

SL002132US
Supplier 03, Date 0412, Print run 1456

Contents

What is a knight?

The **Middle Ages** was a violent period of history. Bands of **brigands** and warriors **plundered** the land. Knights were highly skilled soldiers who swore to protect **medieval nobles.**

Knights were an elite group of soldiers trained to protect wealthy lords and their castles.

Wealthy lords and their castles and land were constantly under threat of attack. So lords surrounded themselves with talented, **loyal** soldiers who would protect them. These soldiers were trained from a young age to be the very best, and they became known as knights. As well as receiving payment from the lord and war **booty** from their battles, knights were often given areas of land by the lords. Knights collected money from the **peasants** who worked the land so that they could buy the expensive armor, weapons, and horses that they needed.

Early knights lived by a simple code. Instead of attacking and pillaging at random, they took pride in fighting in the service of their lord. Eventually, this developed into the set of **values** known as the knight's **Chivalric Code** (see pages 18-19). Because all knights shared the same ideals, they saw themselves as an international brotherhood.

That's an order

Most knights belonged to associations known as orders. The first orders were formed by the church, but later ones were inspired more by **chivalry** than religion. The members of an order swore loyalty to each other and to the king. They often wore a common symbol to identify themselves as part of an order.

The order called the Knights Hospitaller protected Christian pilgrims visiting the **Holy Land**. Members could easily be recognized by the white cross displayed on their black **surcoat**.

Pages and squires

Knights were a cut above the soldiers that made up the castle **garrison**. They were educated and had expert fighting skills. Trainee knights were called pages and squires.

The sons of nobles were often sent to castles at the age of 7 to begin their training. These young **apprentices** were called pages. Pages were taught manners and **etiquette** by the lady of the castle, educated by the **chaplain,** and taught basic **combat** skills by castle soldiers.

Young pages were expected to serve the lord and lady of the castle during meal times. At a banquet such as this, the pages also served the lord's honored guests.

WRITE OR FIGHT?

Early knights were not able to read and write. Their only aim was to beat other knights in battle. However, as the knights' status in society increased, they became much better educated.

At the age of 14 or 15, successful pages were promoted to the position of squire. Each squire served a particular knight and cared for his horses, weapons, and armor. Squires were expected to develop excellent horse-riding and fighting skills. Squires accompanied their knights everywhere, even into battle.

During this modern medieval reenactment a knight and his three squires line up to greet their lord.

A squire hits the quintain's target and narrowly misses being hit by the weight.

Target practice!

Squires spent many hours training with a piece of equipment called the quintain. This was a wooden post with a spinning arm above. The arm had a shield at one end and a weight (such as a bag of stones) hanging from the other. The squire rode up to the quintain and attempted to hit the shield with his lance, sending the quintain spinning. If successful, he had to make a quick getaway or the weight would hit him on the back of the head.

7

Becoming a knight

Once a young squire had proven his bravery and skill, he would become a knight. This usually happened around the age of 21. The knighting ceremony was called dubbing and it was often performed in a castle by a lord.

In this illustration, a squire is being dubbed by the king. Lords could also perform this ceremony.

A variety of skills

As well as being loyal and skillful fighters, squires had to demonstrate a lot of different skills before they could become a knight. For example, they had to be very polite, and able to sing, dance, write poetry, and play popular games, such as chess.

To prepare for the ceremony, the squire would take a long bath to make sure he was clean and pure. After prayers in the chapel, pages would help him dress in his finest clothes.

At the start of the ceremony, the squire approached the lord and knelt before him. Then the lord dubbed him by touching his shoulder with the flat side of a sword. The dubbing was often followed by feasting, music, and dancing.

Bravery rewarded

In times of war, squires were sometimes knighted on the battlefield. This usually happened when the squire had performed an extremely brave act. His knight would then perform the dubbing.

This 14th-century painting shows a brave young squire being dubbed on the battlefield.

MODERN-DAY KNIGHTS

Knights still exist in the UK today (though they do not fight like medieval knights). The government usually decides who should be knighted and the queen dubs them with a sword. As in medieval times, male knights are given the title "Sir." There is a similar ceremony for women where they receive the title "Dame."

Wearing armor

The armor worn by knights changed throughout the Middle Ages to keep pace with the different weapons that were used. Armor was designed to provide maximum protection and movement.

In the 11th and 12th centuries knights wore chain mail made from tiny iron rings that were linked together. This sort of armor was **flexible** and allowed the knight to move freely. However, it also rusted and the links were easily broken.

This early medieval knight wears a chain-mail tunic called a hauberk. Knights often wore a chain-mail hood beneath their helmet to provide extra protection.

Steel plate armor became increasingly popular from the 13th century. Steel plates were first worn over elbows and knees, but eventually suits of armor became common. These suits covered and protected the knight's entire body.

Heavy metal

Knights had to be in good shape to fight while wearing plate armor. A suit of armor weighed around 50 pounds (23 kg), but allowed knights good flexibility of movement. This was very important when faced with an enemy in battle.

A knight could not put on the suit alone, so he relied on squires to arm him. He wore an arming doublet underneath the plates. This was like a padded jacket. It had sections of chain mail to protect places that the plates did not cover, such as under the arms. Each piece of plate armor was put on from the feet upward, secured by leather straps or riveted together. Finally, the upper body plates were attached to the doublet.

Squires attach pieces of plate armor to the doublet of this 15th-century knight.

NEED FOR SPEED

Once the arming doublet was in place, two squires could arm a knight in less than five minutes. They could remove the armor in even less time.

Weapons

There were four main weapons that every medieval knight used. These were the sword, shield, lance, and dagger. Other weapons, such as axes and maces, were sometimes used to defeat an enemy too.

The knight's most important weapon was his sword. Each knight used the same sword throughout his life and often gave it a name. When not in use, the sword was kept in a **sheath** that was fastened around the knight's waist and worn on the left side.

Medieval swords were often made from a mixture of iron and steel, making them tough and flexible with hard cutting edges.

FAMOUS SWORD

The swords of knights sometimes became famous in their own right. For example, Excalibur is the legendary sword of King Arthur and was said to be magical.

The knight's second most valuable weapon was his shield. The shield enabled him to protect himself from an enemy's blows while attacking with his sword. Shields also carried the knight's coat of arms, allowing him to be identified in battle (see pages 14-15).

The lance was a long wooden spear with an iron tip, up to 10 feet (3 m) long. Lances were used by knights on horseback to attack enemies from a distance. They were also used in **jousting** competitions (see pages 16-17).

A knight carries his long, pointed lance as he charges toward an opponent during a jousting competition.

The crossbow and longbow were considered peasant weapons and were never handled by knights. However, they were used to defeat them. Arrows flew at the speed of modern bullets and could **penetrate** chain mail or the joints of plate armor. Another weapon commonly used to defeat knights was the halberd. This long pole had a hook on the end to pull knights from their horses. The halberd also had an ax head that could deliver a **lethal** blow.

Heraldry

All knights looked the same once they were dressed in their armor. So knights displayed symbols or designs, known as coats of arms, on their shields, surcoats, and **standards** to identify themselves.

Knights often took part in competitions called tournaments that were run and scored by men known as heralds. The heralds needed to be able to recognize each knight quickly, to ensure that points were awarded to the correct person. Heralds soon became familiar with the knights' coats of arms and kept records of them. This system, and its rules, became known as heraldry.

The records kept by heralds were called rolls of arms. This is the Hyghalmen Roll which was created in the 15th century in Germany.

A knight chose the symbols that appeared on his coat of arms. His choice often related to a personal experience or to his family. For example, if his family owned farmland, the knight might choose to display a sheaf of wheat. If a shell was included in the design, this often meant that he had been on a **pilgrimage**.

A group of knights enters the showground during a tournament reenactment. Their unique heraldry helps the heralds and spectators to tell one knight from another.

Coats of arms became a symbol of family pride. Eventually they were used on all household items, on flags, and as a seal for important documents.

FAMILY HERALDRY

When noble families married, they combined their coats of arms by dividing the shield. As their children married, it was divided again. This process was called quartering. When a knight's son became a knight himself, he would base his coat of arms upon his father's.

15

Tournaments

Grand contests, known as tournaments, were held, in which knights could show off their fighting skills. Hundreds of knights gathered for the events, which usually lasted several days.

As the competition began, heralds announced the arrival of the knights. Competitors would then parade across the showground wearing full armor and displaying their heraldry. Noble men and women watched the spectacle from a grandstand, while peasants stood or sat on the bare earth.

Knights pitched their colorful tents in a field next to the tournament showground. These events were often sponsored by a local lord who provided the prize money.

Once the **pageantry** was complete, the jousting competition began. In this part of the event, knights on horseback carrying long lances charged at each other. The aim was to unseat your opponent (knock him from his horse). Knights were allowed to break up to three lances in the joust. After that, they would have to continue fighting with swords on foot until one **surrendered**. The weapons used at tournaments were blunted, but even so, knights were often injured.

Splinters of wood fly as a knight's lance hits its target—the shield of his opponent. Unfortunately, on this occasion his rival was not unseated.

The right way

The long wooden fence that separated jousting knights was called the tilt. Competitors always charged down the right side of the tilt. It was introduced to stop unseated knights being trampled by their opponent's horse.

Playing by the rules

The first tournaments were wild and chaotic. Fields of crops were damaged and valuable knights were killed. In 1292, rules were introduced to regulate tournaments, and they became well-organized affairs.

Chivalry

Knights were all supposed to live by a code of good behavior, known as chivalry. As this code developed, knights began to be seen as romantic heroes rather than fierce warriors.

The code of chivalry contained many rules. Knights had to be brave, honest, kind, loyal, and respect their enemies. They were also required to protect and **honor** women. Under the code of chivalry, knights were forbidden to fight one another except in battle. Other strict rules dictated how knights should behave in battle. For example, they were expected to treat their enemies fairly.

The Prince of Wales becomes the first Knight of the Garter in 1348. The Knights of the Garter was the first chivalric order in Britain. The members were chosen by King Edward III.

Chivalry was also closely related to the idea of romance. Each knight chose a lady as the object of his affection and worshipped her from a distance. If the lady approved of him, they would begin a romantic, but distant, courtship. This was known as courtly love. The chosen women were always nobles and were often married, too.

Medieval art and poetry often portrayed knights as romantic heroes. This 19th-century painting was inspired by a 15th-century poem about courtly love.

TOKEN LOVE

During tournaments, knights would often seek tokens, such as handkerchiefs, from their chosen ladies. If successful, the knight would pin the token to his sleeve or tie it around his lance to bring him luck.

The rules of chivalry only applied to nobles. Peasant men and women were often treated brutally by knights.

Battles and tactics

Medieval knights saw war as something brave and heroic. They were often supported in battle by foot soldiers, including archers and crossbowmen.

Sieges were a common type of warfare in the Middle Ages. Large armies would surround a castle and cut off its supplies. They would then either wait for the castle to surrender, or attack it. Once battle commenced, knights would lead the attack, storming the castle walls and fighting off the castle defenders.

In this reenactment, knights have managed to breach the castle walls and are battling with the castle garrison.

WORTH YOUR WEIGHT IN GOLD

Knights and nobles were often captured in battle rather than killed. They were worth a lot more alive than dead as they could be held to **ransom**. Families were usually willing to pay large sums of money for the safe release of such prisoners.

On the battlefield, large ranks of knights, armed and on horseback, were a terrifying sight for foot soldiers and castle garrisons. Tightly packed groups of knights would lower their lances and charge at their enemy. This charge became a powerful war **tactic** and had an effect similar to a steamroller. Respect and chivalry did not apply to peasants or lowly men-at-arms who were often killed without mercy.

Knights approach the battlefield in a reenactment of the 1410 Battle of Grunwald. During the battle, a Polish-Lithuanian force defeated the Teutonic Knights, an order that was **seizing** territory in the region.

Faithful friend

During the Battle of Agincourt in 1415, the English knight, Sir Piers Legge, lay wounded in the mud. His loyal mastiff dog is said to have fought off French soldiers until Legge's squire and servants could reach him. Unfortunately Legge did not survive, but the dog returned to England a hero.

The Crusades

The city of Jerusalem, sacred to both Christians and Muslims, was captured by the latter during the 11th century. Christian European armies launched a campaign to drive Muslim leaders out of the Holy Land. The resulting wars were known as the **Crusades**.

In 1095, Pope Urban II preached the need for Christian knights to launch a holy war, or Crusade. Thousands of knights set off for the Holy Land, determined to free Jerusalem. They successfully recaptured the city in 1099, having fought many battles along the way. However, Jerusalem soon fell back into the hands of the Muslims, and none of the later Crusades were as successful as the first.

Taking the cross

The Crusades were religious wars, and crusading knights were said to have "taken the cross." They often wore the sign of the cross on their clothing as a symbol of their faith. Although the church was forbidden to go to war, the Pope blessed all crusaders.

A crusader sets off for the Holy Land.

This painting shows the taking of Beirut by the crusaders in 1197.

Not all crusaders took up arms for religious reasons. Nobles and knights could see opportunities to extend their power from Europe into the Middle East. The possibility of **acquiring** fame, fortune, and land overseas was very appealing. As the crusaders traveled across the Holy Land, they seized territory and built castles to guard their route. Looting treasure and holding rich enemies to ransom also provided them with income. Many knights were extremely wealthy by the time they returned from the Crusades.

RESPECT YOUR ENEMIES

The Muslim soldiers who defended the Holy Land were called Saracens. Their most famous leader was Saladin. Despite being an enemy, Saladin was respected as a great military leader by many European crusaders.

Family life

Knights weren't always taking part in battles and sieges. They were quite often wealthy, owning houses and land on their lords' **estates**.

Lords valued the knights who were loyal and fought to protect them. They often gave away small areas of their land to the knights and granted them permission to build a house on it. In this way, knights became landowners and were able to demand rent from the peasants who lived and worked there. When home from battle, knights would survey their land, traveling around and checking on the work of the peasants. They might also become involved in local politics and be required to punish lawbreakers.

When a knight was not away fighting, he would enjoy spending time with his family. His sons were often sent away at the age of 7 to begin training as knights.

Despite the tradition of courtly love (see page 19), knights usually had a wife and family at home. They would train their young sons in preparation for their roles as pages in a castle. For entertainment, knights would practice the arts that they had learned, such as writing poetry and singing. Sometimes they would be invited to hunt with the lord, too.

WAR GAME

Chess was a popular game among knights and nobles. It allowed them to practice military tactics. The chess pieces known as knights represent the actual role of these medieval soldiers— to protect the more important pieces, or in real life, the nobles.

The chess pieces called knights often take the form of a horse's head. There are two knights in each player's set.

Knights were always in the service of their lord and could be called away to protect him at any time. Not only did they fight in battles and sieges, they also often acted as bodyguards when the lord traveled across country. They represented their lord when fighting in tournaments as well.

Notable knights

Knights were celebrated as romantic heroes during the medieval period. Some knights even became famous for their brave deeds.

In 1296 Scotland was under the rule of English King Edward I. William Wallace, later known as "Braveheart," led an **uprising** against the invaders. At the Battle of Stirling Bridge in September 1297 Wallace led his army to victory and reclaimed Scotland's freedom. Having become a national hero, Wallace was knighted.

Mel Gibson played Scottish warrior William Wallace in the 1995 epic, *Braveheart*.

Sir Thomas Erpingham was knighted by Lord John of Gaunt, who owned a large estate in Norfolk. He later fought alongside King Henry V at the famous Battle of Agincourt in 1415, in which English forces defeated a much larger French army. Erpingham was immortalized as a character in William Shakespeare's famous play, *Henry V.*

Sir Thomas Erpingham rallies his troops at the Battle of Agincourt in 1415.

A WOMAN AT WAR

The Hundred Years War was a series of long wars between England and France from 1337 to 1453. Joan of Arc was a young peasant girl who believed she had been given a mission by God to free France. She inspired French knights and soldiers to rise up against the English. Unfortunately, in 1431 Joan was taken prisoner by the English, accused of witchcraft, and burned at the stake.

Joan of Arc leads her troops to victory during the siege of Orléans in 1429.

Knights in myth and legend

During the medieval period myths and legends about knights and their battles were common. Many of these stories are still famous today.

One of the most well-known legends featuring knights is the story of King Arthur and the **Knights of the Round Table**. The tale developed through the Middle Ages as it was told and written down by different storytellers. The version we know today features many famous knights including Lancelot, who fell in love with King Arthur's wife Guinevere, and his son Galahad, who was described as the "perfect knight" and joined the **quest** for the **Holy Grail**.

This painting shows the legendary King Arthur and his Knights of the Round Table.

Saint George is believed to have lived in the 3rd century. However, he is famous in legend as being a knight who fought and killed a great dragon in order to save a princess. The story spread during the 15th century and was printed in a book called *The Golden Legend* in 1483.

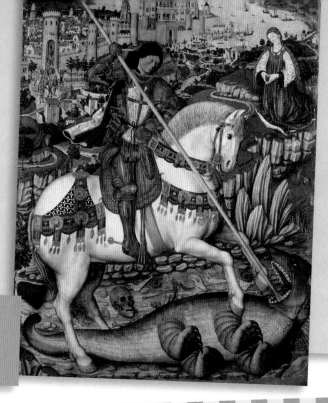

A 15th-century painting shows Saint George fighting the dragon. The princess watches from a distance.

KNIGHT OR NOT?

Robin Hood was a legendary outlaw who robbed the rich to feed the poor. Some believe that this character may have been based on the real-life knight named Robert Fitzwalter. However, Hood was a talented archer, a skill unlikely to be found in a knight.

This statue of Robin Hood stands in front of Nottingham Castle.

The Canterbury Tales is a collection of stories written by Geoffrey Chaucer at the end of the 14th century. One of the stories, *The Knight's Tale*, tells of two young knights who fall in love with the same maiden. The former friends become enemies and battle to decide which one will marry her. The 2001 movie *A Knight's Tale* was partly based on this story.

Glossary

acquire to get or obtain something

apprentice a person who is learning a trade

booty stolen treasure

breach to break through something

brigand a member of a gang that robs people

chaplain the person in charge of religious life in a castle

Chivalric Code the code of good behavior that knights were expected to live by

chivalry the behavior of an ideal knight

combat fighting

Crusades wars between Christians and Muslims that took place in the 11th, 12th and 13th centuries

estate a large area of land that is owned by one person

etiquette the rules of polite behavior

flexible able to bend without breaking

garrison a group of soldiers who defend a castle

Holy Grail a cup or platter said to have been used by Jesus Christ, which was searched for by knights in the legend of King Arthur

Holy Land a Middle Eastern region, in what is now Israel and Palestine, that is sacred to Jews, Muslims, and Christians

honor to treat with respect

jousting a competition between two knights fighting on horseback with lances

Knights of the Round Table the order of knights featured in the legend of King Arthur

lethal deadly

loyal faithful to someone or something

medieval describes the period of the Middle Ages in Europe from the 5th to the 15th centuries

Middle Ages the medieval period of history, between the 5th century and the 15th century

noble someone who has a high social rank, such as a lord, lady, duke, or baron

pageantry a colorful display

peasants people who worked on a lord's land; the lowest class in medieval times

penetrate to break through

pilgrim a person who makes a journey (called a pilgrimage) to a sacred place

plunder to use force to steal things

quest a long or difficult search for something

ransom an amount of money demanded for the release of a prisoner

reenactment the acting out of an historical event

seize to take something by force

sheath a cover for a blade or sword

standard a flag carried on a pole

surcoat a tunic or robe worn over armor

surrender to stop fighting and agree that the other side has won

tactic a plan to achieve success

uprising an act of rebellion or revolt

values a set of important beliefs

Further reading

Exploring Ancient Civilizations: Medieval Times by Robynne Eagan (Teaching & Learning, 2002)

Knights and Castles (Navigators) by Philip Steele (Kingfisher, 2011)

Knights and Warriors by Aaron Ralby (Hammond, 2009)

Life as a Knight by Rachel Hanel (Capstone, 2010)

The Medieval Knight by Christoher Gravett (Brighter Child, 2001)

Medieval Knights by Charlotte Guillain (Raintree, 2010)

Want to be a Knight? by Paul Mason (Crabtree, 2001)

Web sites

www.childrensmuseum.org/castles/games.php
Make your own coat of arms and play fun games in the Lego Castle Adventure.

http://www.kingarthursknights.com
Find out all about King Arthur and his legendary knights on this informative web site.

http://www.royalarmories.org/home
Learn all about medieval armor at the Royal Armories web site.

http://www.tudorbritain.org/joust
Try to keep your knight on his horse in this fun jousting game.

Index